CIRCLES IN THE SAND

By Philip Macht
Illustrated by Robert Seyffert
Music by Robert Macht

Maxrom Press/Baltimore

for Eloise and Danny

☆   ☆   ☆   ☆   ☆   ☆

Text copyright © 1984 by Philip Macht
Illustrations copyright © 1985 by Robert Seyffert
Music copyright © 1984 by Robert Macht
All rights reserved

Library of Congress Card Catalog Number: 84-90597
ISBN: 0-930339-00-2

Published in the United States by:
Maxrom Press, 11 E. Fayette Street
Baltimore, Maryland 21202

Printed in the U.S.A.   First Edition

CIRCLES

IN

THE

SAND

Chapter One _____

It was a normal day in the wilderness. The tribe had been wandering since sunrise, looking for their promised land, as they had for years since The Great Escape—when Max led them out of their terrible troubles down south.

On most days, they wandered from sunrise to sunset just to find enough grazing for the flocks.

Occasionally, when the rains came, the hills and plains would green up as if by magic, and the tribe could rest. But they were usually on the move.

Donkeys carried the tents, grain, wool, water, wine and other heavy stuff. Max rode the camel. Everyone else walked, except the pregnant women and little babies—Max was careful about them.

All the years of wandering were hard on old folks—they faded away. They may have given up hope that Max would ever find the right promised land. In fact, Max was the only really old old person left. Though he didn't show it when he danced and played the ram's horn. Or when he traded with passing caravans.

Wandering was tiresome for almost everyone except the children. The children could run ahead of the tribe and play, or they could help with the sheep and goats, or they could climb the hills to look for promised lands. They could walk along with the good singers and learn the words to the old songs.

The children did have to be careful not to bother Max. That wasn't much of a problem on the trail—Max had learned to sleep on his camel during the day so he could keep an eye on the tribe at night, and sing and dance and lead the evening activities.

It didn't take much to entertain the tribe. They were so glad to stop after a day's wandering, to make dinner and cool off—almost anything would have been sufficient. But Max didn't coast on that—he worked up something almost every night: Mondays they had songs, Tuesdays they had dancing, Wednesdays they had skits. On Friday nights Max spoofed them with stories about the one and only Spoof.

The tribe used to have many Spoofs; but as Max grew older he couldn't keep straight which Spoof was the Spoof of what, so he simplified things. This new unified Spoof was an efficient idea, but not much fun; and every once in a while when Max would go up the mountain for a breather, the tribe would backslide into the old ways. If Max caught them at it when he came down, he really lost his sense of humor. He'd smash idols and threaten to smash a few heads.

Those were the only times Max got violent. Generally, he led the tribe by the force and fertility of his personality.

On this particular afternoon, a girl named Sara and her brother Joey were hunting lizards. They were way out in front of the tribe, but they weren't worried about getting lost. One could always see the tribe for miles away—the goats and sheep kicked up so much dust that the tribe always traveled under a cloud.

Sara and Joey found a place of huge rocks. It was a good place to play hiding games in the shade while waiting for the tribe.

The first people up the trail were Uncle Norman and Cousin Ben. (Almost everyone in the tribe was some kind of uncle, aunt or cousin). Norman and Ben were puffing hard. When they got to the shade of the rocks, they put down their packs and canteens and guitars, and flopped to the ground.

"This is it, Ben," Norman said. "We'll just tell Max we've had enough promised-land-searching for one day."

"Max won't buy it," Ben said.

"What's the rush, Benny? I mean where are we going really?"

"Max always gets upset if we try to quit before sundown."

"I'm hot," Norman whined. "I'm bone tired. My feet hurt. They've been hurting for years."

"Forty years."

"What?"

"Forty years," Ben repeated.

"Is it really forty years?"

"Sure, Norman, since we were kids. Since The Great Escape. All this time looking for our own P.L."

"You know, we've seen a lot of P.L.'s in the distance these years."

"Yeah," Ben said. "Bet we've passed up some good bets. Like the one all week off to the west."

"It sure looks promising."

"I asked Max about it: 'Maybe it's ours, Max', I said."

"What did he say, Ben?"

"What he always says: 'Wrong one again, peon'. He hardly looked. I wish he'd stop calling us 'peons'. Why does he have to always call us 'peons'?"

"Because we are," Norman said.

"Why?"

"Because we've been following *him* around for forty years."

"Well why do we do it?"

"He's got us spoofed."

Sara put her hand over Joey's mouth—he was giggling so hard. Uncle Norman and Cousin Ben had this same conversation all the time. And they weren't the only ones. Most of the grown-ups did some grumbling on the trail these years.

Norman picked at his guitar. Ben took a few nips from his red canteen. After a minute or two, Ben asked, "Norman, how come we're the tribe to get spoofed?"

"We were chosen. Spoof chose us. Spoof chose us peons to be his favorite tribe of peons."

"*You* don't have to keep calling us *peons*," Ben said.

"And Spoof chose Max to lead us. That's the story."

Ben took another nip from his red canteen and a long drink from his blue one. He put his knapsack under his head for a pillow, looked up at the sky, and very casually asked, "You still believe in Spoof as much as you used to?"

"What's on your mind, Ben?" Norman asked.

"I'm beginning to have my doubts is all."

"Starting when?"

"Five, maybe six years ago."

"Yeah?"

"I started to think. I mean how do we *know*? How do we really know?" Ben asked.

"Yeah, I know the feeling."

"How do we know there's only *one* Spoof . . . and what about all that business that we can't see Him."

"Yeah."

"We used to have a lot of Spoofs. Some nice ones, too."

"Real nice." Norman agreed.

"Remember the bronze one shaped like a camel with ten humps? What was his name?"

"Hump."

"Hump?"

"Yeah, 'Hump'. There were ten humps and each hump meant something."

"See, that's what I mean," Ben said. "You could *see* the humps. It was believable."

"How about when we had a real cow for one?"

"We ate her." Ben stood up. He walked out of the shade. He pointed up at the sun and said, "Speaking of Spoofs! Other people's Spoofs I mean—you've got to admit the people down south had a hot one!"

"Ha. Ha."

"Well, the sun is a great idea, even if it is *theirs*."

"I wouldn't want it," Norman said. "I don't want their Spoof, or anything else to remind me of them." He strummed his guitar hard for emphasis . . . "How about when we carried that big yellow rock around? What ever happened to it?"

"We sold it . . . See what I mean. With all those other Spoofs you could see them, or feel them, . . . or sell them. But now with our one and only Spoof—nothing." Ben closed his eyes.

"Max can hear him," Norman said. "Spoof speaks to Max, and Max can hear and give us peons the word."

"Yeah, but *we* can't hear him. It's spoofy."

"Very spoofy."

Sara and Joey slipped out from behind the rocks as though they had just come up the trail.

"Hi, kids," Norman said. "How's it going?"

"Swell, Uncle Norman," Sara said. "Nice shady spot here."

"Play us a song, Uncle Norman," Joey said.

Norman tuned up and started humming "The Peon's Lament". Then after a while he sang the words.

THE PEON'S LAMENT

"I can't believe it's still happening,
Can't believe in all this rock and sand
we can't find our little place,
Our always promised promised-land.

      Oh our poor back is breaking,
      Oh our poor feet are sore,
      And we got this funny feeling,
      And we got this awful feeling
      We been by this place before.

I can't believe it's still happening,
Can't believe that every day's the same,
Wandering 'round in wilderness,
Busting our bones on this plain.

      Oh our poor back is breaking,
      Oh our poor feet are sore,
      And we got this funny feeling,
      And we got this awful feeling
      We been by this place before!

The Peon's Lament

Oh, our poor feet are sore,

And we got this fun - ny feel - ing,

And we got this aw - ful feel - ing, We been by

_ this place _ be - fore.

x

Other people straggled in, relaxed in the shade, and joined the singing. They sang for about an hour before they saw Max humping along on his camel.

"Okay, guys," someone said, "better break it up and get moving. Here he comes."

People moaned and groaned.

"Hold it!" Uncle Norman shouted. "Hold it right there! Me and Benny here have been thinking. Right, Ben?"

"Right, Norman."

"We've been thinking we've had enough for today. This is a good spot to camp. Got some shade and a nice view. Only a few more hours to sunset anyway. Why don't we quit for the day? Why?"

Someone shouted, "Max is why."

" . . . So?" Norman said. "We've got rights. Right, Ben?"

Ben hesitated.

"Right, Benny???" Norman's voice was screechy.

" . . . Right," Ben whispered.

"There! Ben is with me. Now, who's next?"

Silence.

"Well, how about it?" Norman said. "Speak up!"

A few hands went up. Then more. Then all. Norman and a few other good players struck up a lively tune, and the others hustled about unloading the donkeys and breaking out the tents.

Sara and Joey rushed over to their Mom and Dad. They were excited! What a happening! They hugged and kissed Mom and Dad.

"What do you think, Dad?" Sara asked.

Dad smiled. "Sounds like Norman's red canteen speaking."

"Think we have a chance to get away with it?" Joey asked.

"Sure, Joey," Mom cut in, "about as much chance as a duck in a desert."

The rest of the tribe wandered in along with the sheep and the donkeys and the pregnant women and babies. Last came Max, still asleep on his camel. The camel walked to the center and stopped.

That woke Max up. He yawned, looked around him, and slowly shook his ancient head.

"Nice place, huh Max?" someone said casually.

Max smiled at the tribe settling in. He wasn't angry; he knew their tricks. "Nice *try*," he said, "Now saddle up."

Norman stood up on a rock. "Gosh, Max, . . . er . . . this is a good spot. Look: a little shade, a little stubble for the flocks over on the hill, a breeze, and a super view from up here of the promised land."

"*A* promised land," Max corrected.

" . . . but Max . . . " Norman pleaded.

"Wrong one again, peon."

"But, Max, look . . . there's a lake out there."

The tribe sighed.

"And a little river running into it."

The tribe sighed again.

"And green all along the river."

The tribe oohed and aahed.

"Probably got date trees, and—"

"—Come on down, Norman," Max said. "You've been out in the sun too long."

Ben popped up: "How about we send a scout out for a look?"

"Knock if off, Benny," Max said. "Okay, peons, the party's over. There's a good camp site in three hours, with a well and big cliffs for shade."

But no one moved.

"Okay, all together now," Max cheered, "hit the trail—let's move it!"

Still no one moved.

Max's face hardened. He walked his camel through the crowd without looking at anyone. With great ceremony, he dismounted, climbed the biggest rock, and raised his arms to the sky. "OH, SPOOF," he thundered in the voice he saved for such occasions, "OH, SPOOF, WHAT AM I GOING TO DO WITH THESE STUBBORN PEOPLE?!"

The tribe froze at the mention of Spoof.

Max closed his eyes as if he were listening for an answer from the sky. He nodded his head. "Uh huh, uh huh," he whispered respectfully, " . . . sure thing, . . . uh huh."

Then he looked everyone in the eye—all at the same time. "*He* says if you all don't start moving like I say, *He* may just think *He* chose the wrong tribe!"

The people grumbled; but they started loading up.

Max smiled and shrugged. "I'm only telling you what He is telling me," he said in his sweetest voice. "I'm only telling you what He is telling me."

That was his cue to the musicians to play, and Max sang his famous marching song:

Max's Famous Marching Song

"Onward, my brothers,
we've made a good start.
Forward, my brothers,
now let's not lose heart.

That land that we passed
—just not your spot.
I told you before
but you peons forgot.

Up now, my cousins,
night is for sleep.
We can have dancing,
we'll kill us a sheep.

I am your leader,
that's how it has to be,
Now that you all are—
Now that you all are free.

I'm only telling you,
what Spoof is telling me.
I'm only telling you
what He is telling me.

He says keep looking
for your promised land.
I'll know how it looks,
—not too much sand.

The water is sweet,
Fruit on the trees,
There's always some grass,
Oh and sometimes a breeze.

We can have chickens,
We'll buy a cow.
Up now my cousins
Don't quit on me now.

But the tribe
didn't move out
and Max got upset
again.

I am your leader!
That's how it has to be!
Now that you peons—
Now that you all are free!

I'm only telling you
what Spoof is telling me!
I'm only telling you
what He is telling me!

That got them moving.
Max stopped singing.
He raised his arms to
the sky and boomed:

Woe to the peons
who won't follow Spoof!
There teeth will fall out
their donkeys will droop!

Their goats will go thin,
their heads will go fat!
You better believe
He knows where you're at!

Woe to the peons
who won't follow Him,
Their boys will be short,
their girls will be thin!

19

The sun will stand still!
The sky will be black!
The wine will go sour!
The bread will be flat!

It will rain beetles . . .
and snakes on your hair!
Your beard will grow short,
your tent will be bare!

Your kids won't inquire,
they will be simple!
Their teeth won't be straight,
their freckles will pimple!

They'll rough up your goats,
They'll lose your best sheep!
They'll talk back sassy . . .
And not go to sleep . . . !

He was still screaming at them
long after they could make out
the actual words.

. . . SAND IN YOUR LUNGS!
. . . SPEAKING IN TONGUES!
. . . WHY CAN'T YOU PEONS SEE
I'M ONLY TELLING YOU
WHAT HE IS TELLING ME!

Max's Famous Marching Song

Moderato, forcefully

On-ward, my broth-ers, we've made a good start. For-ward, my broth-ers, now___
He says keep look-ing for your prom-ised land. I'll___ know how it looks, not___

___ let's not lose heart. That land that___ we passed___ just not your spot.
___ too much sand. The wat-er___ is sweet,___ fruit on the trees,

I told you be - fore but you pe - ons___
There's al - ways some grass, Oh, and some-times___

for - got. Up now, my cous - ins, Night is for sleep.___
a breeze. We can have chick - ens, We'll buy a cow.___

We can have danc-ing, we'll kill us a sheep.
Up now my cous-ins, Don't quit on me now. } I am your lead-er!

That's how it has to be,
{ Now that you all are,
{ Now that you pe-ons,
Now that you all are free!
Now that you all are free!

I'm on-ly tell-ing you what Spoof is tell-ing me! I'm on-ly tell-ing you

what He is tell-ing me. me.

That was some sad tribe—trudging along in little family groups, heads down, kicking up more dust than usual.

Sara and Joey were walking with Mom and Dad. Dad looked at Mom out of the corner of his eye and said, "All right, honey, don't say it."

"I didn't say a word, Dave," Mom said.

"But you're thinking."

"You know it!"

"Come on, Rosie, what do you want from me?"

"The whole lot of you! Folded right up like a silk tent in a sandstorm."

" . . . *You* didn't say anything."

"Me?" Mom said, " . . . Me?? . . . Want me to embarrass you in front of your friends?"

It was glum.

After a while, Mom said, "Cousin Ben was right! We should scout that P.L. down there with the river and the lake." She looked Dad straight in the eye. "It's *time* we found something out for ourselves! Did something for ourselves!"

"What good would it do?" Dad sulked.

"Look, Dave, if we knew for sure, . . . if we really knew it was an okay place . . . Doesn't have to be perfect."

" . . . So?"

"So, we could go there. Then it would be ours. Max never said it has to be perfect. That's not the promise. Just has to be ours. That's the promise."

"You're making me nervous," Dad said.

"Good. Maybe you'll do something. Somebody's got to do something soon. This wilderness is getting to us. We're as uptight as a ram in December."

"Max will never—"

—"for Spoof's sake, man!" Mom said. "Will you stop shaking in your sandals. You're not going to *ask* Max. Just sneak a scout out to see what's down there."

Mom studied the tribe around her. She wrinkled her forehead in her study look. She looked right at Sara. "Sara!" she said, "Sara and Joey! They can do it, Dave. It's a natural. They can drift over with the flocks and slip away. Get down there by midnight tonight, and check the place out tomorrow. Catch up with us next day."

Dad's mouth hung open.

Mom rolled right along: "Don't worry; they won't get lost—Sara knows the stars. And they'll know what to look for down there: Joey knows a little about grass and trees, Sara knows something about rivers and lakes and–"

–"And fish!" Sara said.

"And I know dates," Joey said, "and soil and . . . we can do it, Dad!"

"We can!" Sara agreed. "I can't believe we can't!"

"Give them a chance, Dave," Mom said. "Give them a chance for a better life than we had. You don't want your children always walking around under a cloud."

Dad hugged his children to him. His eyes were misty.

"Go on, kids," Mom said. "Get your things. Take water, some cheese, some dates. Dad'll be okay." She kissed them. "And take your sling shots." (Dad moaned). "And take your heavy blankets for the night."

Chapter Two

Sara and Joey slipped away easily. They headed toward a bend in the river, a little above where it flowed into the lake.

By sundown, they guessed they were halfway there. They stopped to rest and eat.

Then they hurried on under the stars. It was a cool, sparkling night; but with just a quarter moon, it was almost dark on the plain.

Every so often, Sara stopped to check the sky: to check the North Star; and to look for the other stars she knew.

About three hours later, they heard water trickling. They were on top of a narrow rocky gorge with a spring feeding the river. That's where the children slept.

At sunrise, they saw the deer. Along the rim of the gorge, and scattered along the rocky ledge walls, there were delicate little deer: maybe twenty. The deer were wary. When the children moved, the deer scrambled over the rocks. They jumped from rock to rock easily, gracefully—as if each deer had a proper spot to aim for on each rock.

That showed Joey and Sara the way down, though *they* didn't do any rock-jumping. They found the little spring. The water was almost cold! Around the spring were thick reeds about twice as tall as Sara.

The slope was gentle from the spring on down, and it was no more than a careful walk from there to the river.

Sara and Joey waded into the marshes. Sara stopped still. "Look, Joey," she whispered, "look at this school." Hundreds of little fish, about an inch long, swam by and then turned, all together in one motion, and swam away.

"Too bad," Joey said, "Can't get fat on them."

Sara looked pained.

"Okay," Joey shrugged, "so tell me."

"Big fish eat little fish. Little fish here means big fish out in the river, and bigger fish in the lake! Fantastic! This is a fantastic P.L.!" She ran along the marshes exploring and hollering back: "Frogs!", and then "Snails!". And a lot more "fantastics!"

Joey walked along the bank in the other direction, downstream toward the lake. He saw thickets of willow trees, and a few gum trees wide enough to make good boards for boats. He saw deer tracks coming down to the river. Sara is right, Joey thought, this is fantastic!

Joey waited for Sara in a grove of date palms at the head of the lake. The lake was the most wonderful sight of all: blue and shimmering—little waves breaking on the beach. And he could not see the far end!

When Joey saw Sara coming through the woods, he ran to meet her.

They were so excited they couldn't stop talking—telling of all they had seen. They spent the rest of the day exploring together. By sunset they were exhausted. They made a fire in a clearing in the woods near the lake, ate supper, and rolled up in their blankets.

But Sara was too excited to sleep.

"Joey," Sara whispered, "this must be the place."

" . . . Hmmm," Joey mumbled.

"I can't wait to tell Mom and Dad."

" . . . Hmmm."

"I just can't believe that Max won't believe that this is not the place."

" . . . You've got a way with words, Sara."

"Just think," she said, "in this land we could have big tents, or even mud houses like oasis tribes have. I could have a room of my own."

"Hmmm."

"Joey, we could have a school. And we could go every day."

"Every day?"

"Well almost every day," Sara compromised.

"Girls will go to school?"

"Sure, Joey, in the promised land I can't believe that girls won't be equal."

"Hmmm."

"What's wrong with that?" she said. "Suppose you were a girl?"

"I can't believe that you can't believe that I can't pretend I'm a girl."

"See, that's the problem—men have no imagination . . . In the P.L., girls are going to be equal. So, what do you say to that?"

"It's *your* story."

"And . . . and . . . ," Sara said, "we'll be allowed to pick our own husbands."

"Boys don't even get to pick. They're not complaining."

"See, that's the problem—men have no imagination."

"Hmmm."

"Hmmm."

" . . . hmmmm."

" . . . hmmmmmzzz"

" . . . . . . zzzzzzzzzz"

Chapter Three

In the middle of the night, Sara had a terrible dream: she was surrounded by shadow figures holding long spears. The spear tips glistened in the firelight.

The shadows were silently closing in—closer and closer. Sara pulled the blanket over her head. She shook herself . . . Whew!

When her head was clear, she peeked out. The spears were still there! "No! No!," she screamed. "Go away! This is a dream!"

The shadows laughed deep men's laughs. They pounced on Sara and Joey, tied their hands, and gagged them. Terror! Terror! Joey's eyes were wild with terror. Sara trembled violently. The children moaned and struggled as the men dragged them out of the clearing.

The men had hidden camels in the woods. Each child was placed on a camel with one of the men. Then the other men mounted up and moved out, single file—still without speaking. The only sounds were the footsteps and the breathing of the camels.

Joey couldn't see the men's faces clearly. Who are they? Where are they taking us? What will they do to us? He thought about the old stories of slavery.

Sara tried to concentrate on the route. She watched the stars. She figured they were heading south, paralleling the shore of the lake.

Hours later, they came out of the woods. In the distance, there was the flicker of fires and the outlines of tents. They were approaching a village. One of the men galloped ahead.

Then they passed by flocks of sheep and goats.

It was daybreak.

Joey saw, as they entered the village, that these were not the tents of wandering people. These tents were large, with long thick poles holding the sides and longer poles holding a high roof. The troop dismounted in front of the largest tent. With a man holding each arm, Sara and Joey were led inside. Men in fine robes were seated on raised platforms around the sides of the tent. The man on the highest platform signaled the guards; the children's hands were untied, their gags were removed.

Joey and Sara cried out: "—didn't do anything!"

"—didn't take anything!"

"—didn't hurt anything!"

"—we were lost is all!"

The Head Man laughed. "Get a load of these kids, will you! They talk just like us!"

"Yeah, Nates," said the man next to the Head Man, "and they *look* just like us!"

"Where you from, kids?" Nates asked.

"We're from the wilderness," Sara said. "To the east."

"Don't have to tell us where the wilderness is. Huh, Sid?"

The men laughed like that was the biggest joke in the world.

Sid said, "Wilderness, huh? Max's crew?"

"Yes, Sir," Joey answered, coming back to life.

"That man still kicking? I don't believe it."

"Yes, Sir."

"The same old Max that sings and dances? . . . Always making promises? . . . *that* one?"

"That's Max," Joey said.

Nates sang: " 'I'm only telling you what He is telling me'?? *That* one?"

Everyone in the tent laughed again. Nates and Sid did a jig imitating Max.

They danced over to Sara and Joey. They twirled them around. Soon the whole tent was dancing—dancing and laughing.

Women and children from the camp came in to join the action. "What's happening?" they asked.

Nates got back up on his platform. He signaled for quiet. "These here kids, the foreigners. . . . . that the patrol picked up last night . . . . these kids——THEY'RE YOUR COUSINS!"

"Cousins!" everyone shouted.

"Our cousins!" everyone cheered.

"Then," Sara said. . . . "then you're The Lost Tribe?"

"Lost?!" Nates roared. "Us lost? Do *we* look lost?"

"No, Sir," Joey said.

"Just call me Uncle Nates."

"Yes, Uncle Nates," Joey said.

"And I'm Sara, Joey here is my brother."

"Hmm," Nates said, "Sara and Joey who? Who's your mom and dad?"

"Rosie and Dave."

"Rosie and Dave!" Sid cut in. "You're Rosie and Dave's kids? Then I'm your *real* Uncle Sid. Rosie's my sister! How's she doing these years?"

"Tired," Sara said, "Our whole tribe's tired."

"They ought to be tired," Nates said, "following Max around all these years. We know that drill. We split twenty years ago."

"Twenty-one," someone shouted.

Nates thought about that. " . . . Let's see. Hmmm. My grandma died when she was eighty. So that makes twenty years."

"No," Sid said, "*my* grandma was forty-one at the time of The Great Escape. And it was at night, so that makes twenty-one."

"Well how old was she when she died?" Nates asked.

"For Spoof's sake!" Sid yelled at Nates, "Grandma's sitting right there!"

Sara and Joey stared at each other at the mention of Spoof. They had been wondering about that.

" . . . Er . . . ah . . . . Uncle Nates," Sara asked, " . . . you have Spoof here?"

"Spoof? . . . Sure, why not? No problem. We built Him a nice House. Stone. Down by the lake. And we put Woody in charge. We all give a tenth to The House—a tenth of the dates, a tenth of the lambs,–"

–"and Spoof *eats*?" Joey asked.

"Woody eats. Woody and his helpers. No problem. What's the question?"

Sara looked at Joey. Joey looked at Sara. "Does Spoof *speak* to Woody?" Sara asked.

"Not if He can help it," Sid said. " . . . No, I'm only joking. Truth is we don't go there too much. Maybe a couple days a year. It's for them that likes it, if you know what I mean."

"We do go down for weddings and funerals and such," Nates said. "Woody does all that. And *we* run the tribe. It's better this way, if you know what I mean . . . Hey! You kids must be hungry and thirsty!" Nates snapped his fingers. "Let's take care of our young cousins!" He put his arms around Sara and Joey, and led them up on his platform as guests of honor.

"Tell us," Sid said, "how did you two get so lost?"

Sara blushed. "Well, . . . er . . . ah . . . we really weren't lost. We knew where we were—we just didn't know *you* were here."

"We were scouting," Joey said.

"Scouting?" Nates asked.

"For our promised land."

"Max sent you?"

"No. Mom and Dad sent us. We slipped away."

"They were hoping . . . ," Sara said sadly, " . . . they were hoping this might be our own P.L. . . . "

No one said a word.

The tent was still.

Then the food came, and some talk started up, and people came up to say hello. Soon it was a party—Sara and Joey telling how things were in the wilderness, and their new cousins telling about life by the lake. Oh it sounded good!

After a while, Sid took Sara and Joey to his tent. The sun was high now. Almost everyone in the tribe took a solid three hour nap.

In the afternoon, all the children went swimming and played games and showed toys; and the grown-ups sat around and smoked and played cards. No one did any work—Woody had declared the day a holiday. That was one of Woody's long suits—holidays.

At sundown, Sid's children took Sara and Joey to see The Stone House and to meet Woody in person.

Woody was a funny looking little man—always seemed to be looking back over his own shoulder.

All he wanted to talk about was Max: "Max have any good new prayers?" he asked, and "What's Max say when the plebes get out of line?"

" 'Plebes'?" Joey asked.

" 'Plebes' . . . 'proles' . . . 'peasants' . . . 'peons'," Woody explained.

"Oh," Sara laughed. "He sings, 'Oh woe to the peons who won't follow Spoof'. Then he screams out all the terrible things that will happen if we don't."

"Like what?"

"Like sour wine and teeth falling out and pimples."

"Does he do snakes and locusts?" Woody asked.

"Snakes and beetles."

" . . . Not *locusts*?"

"No, Sir," Sara answered.

"Hmm. Does he do anything with the next life? I mean like after you die?"

"Not really."

"Hmmm. I'm working on an idea there myself. I'm thinking of making a few definite promises."

"Yes, Sir," Joey said.

Woody stared at Joey. "You're sure now? You're sure Max isn't into that?"

"No, Sir. We're still on the promised land promise."

"Good." Woody relaxed.

After that, Woody was very friendly. He even unlocked the doors to the store rooms and showed off his stash. He had everything from grain and skins and dried fish to broken tools and wasted dolls. "Don't know what I'll do with some of this junk," he said, "but . . . you never know what might grab the next caravan."

Woody blessed them when they left:
> "Keep these kids safe,
>   May life be a feast,
>   Keep these kids straight,
>   And tell Max to turn east."

The tribe had another party that night. But just a supper party because Sara and Joey had to head back to the wilderness in the morning.

Nates woke them at daybreak. "Kiss your new cousins before you go", he said. "Then I'll walk you out of town." He gave them a camel for their trip.

After many a sad "goodbye" and "see you around" and "peace/peace", Sara and Joey were alone with Uncle Nates at the edge of the lake-land.

"Listen," Nates said, trying to look casual, " . . . we . . . er . . . we had a little meeting last night after you kids went to bed . . . and . . . and you can tell Rosie and Dave if they want to, you all and your whole tribe can come on down. I mean, there's plenty of land farther down the lake, and we can help you get started."

Oh! Oh, Spoof! That was Sara's wish and Joey's wish! But they weren't sure it had really come true.

Nates winked at them. "After all," he said, "what are cousins for?"

Then they knew it! THEY HAD FOUND THEIR P.L.!

They smothered Uncle Nates with hugs and kisses and tears. Nates was teary, too. He got very busy helping them up on the camel.

Joey shouted, "Camel, make tracks!", and he and Sara trotted off into the sunrise.

Chapter Four

Sara steered the camel on a northeast course that would intercept the tribe, if the tribe had kept wandering north.

It was blazing hot, and uphill all the way; but Sara and Joey were too excited to care—and camels never care about anything.

They kept moving all day. By late afternoon, they saw the outline of high cliffs in the distance. Beyond the cliffs, they saw the cloud the tribe always travels under. As they approached the cliffs, they could make out tiny figures on top, waving.

Joey urged the camel on. By the time they could see the narrow opening in the cliff face, Mom and Dad were running through the pass to meet them.

"What happened?!" Mom shouted. "Your Dad was all worried—look at him."

Sara said, "Ma, we–"

–"You're a whole day late!"

"Ma, we–"

–"Your poor Dad feels lower than a pregnant snake."

"Ma! We found it!" Joey shouted. "We found the promised land!"

"It's fantastic!" Sara cried, "it's got trees and grass and fish–"

–"Hold on," Mom said. "Come on down and kiss your Mom—then I want to hear about it grain by grain."

"And Ma . . ." Joey laughed, " . . . it's got a big surprise. It's–"

–"Wait Joey, wait–"

–"IT'S GOT PEOPLE!"

"People??" Dad asked, worried.

"People, Dad—just like us! Uncle Nates and Real Uncle Sid and"–

–"My brother Sid?" Mom asked.

Joey shook his head yes.

"Rosie," Dad said, "they found The Lost Tribe!"

Sara laughed. "They don't look at it that way, Dad."

"Well," Mom said, "that Sid always was contrary."

"And, Mom, they built this Stone House down by the lake for Spoof. And for Woody."

" 'Woody'? Mom asked. "Did you say 'Woody'? . . . What's he look like?"

"Not much," Sara said.

"Little man; looks like a wounded weasel? Woody? *He* talks to Spoof?"

"Maybe not *talks*, Mom, but he is important. He's got a tenth of everything stored right there in The Stone House."

"Dave," Mom said, "you hear that! Woody! Always looked like he lived under a rock."

"You were sweet on him once." Dad winked at Sara and Joey. Mom blushed. "Was not."

"His folks just didn't have enough goats and sheep for your folks. It's true, kids," Dad said, "Woody never looked like much, but he was always a smooth talker—and I guess he still is."

They saw Uncle Norman and Cousin Ben waving at them frantically from inside the pass.

"Take cover, take cover," Norman called, "Max is awake."

They all raced for the shelter of the pass. There Sara and Joey told of their adventure. They described the promised land, and told what Uncle Nates said about helping the tribe get started.

When Mom was satisfied (about three tellings later), she sent Benny for some important people, and made Sara and Joey tell their tale again.

"Look at my poor tired babies," Mom said, " . . . they look as beat as a ram in March," and she shooed Joey and Sara off to bed so the grown-ups could have a serious meeting.

Norman found a rock to stand on. Everyone gathered in close. "Well?" Norman asked, "anybody here got any doubts? Will we ever find a better P.L.?"

"This is it!" Benny said.

"Dave's for it!" Mom said.

"Let's do it!" everyone shouted, "let's tell Max!"

They started running.

But before they got halfway through the pass, Norman slowed down. "Wait . . . wait . . . " he puffed, "not . . . so . . . fast."

The others thought Norman was just out of shape: "Come on, Norman," they shouted, "run a little!"

"Hold on . . . wait up," Norman said, "let's talk . . . I'm thinking maybe Max won't be too happy about this. Maybe he'll just say, 'Wrong one again, peons', again."

Mom shook Norman by the shoulders. "Get a hold on yourself. He can't say that. We know it's the right one—my brother Sid is there."

"Listen, Rosie," Dad said. "Maybe Norman's got something. How do we know Max will like the idea of settling down? I mean what will he *do* there?"

Benny scratched his head. "Max is awful old to learn new ways."

"That's what I mean," Norman said. "He's been leading us around so long—how will he handle it down there? And then there's Woody. Wait'll he hears about Woody!"

"Hmm."

"Hmm."

The thought of Woody made everybody think.

Then Mom said, "So what! If we're all together, Max can't stop us!"

"Spoof can," Norman said. "Max could tell Spoof, and Spoof could stop us if He wanted."

That even stopped Mom. For a minute. "So? . . . So all that means is Max can't know. We won't tell him! We'll have a big party tonight. We'll really whoop it up like Max always wants us to. Make him sing and dance every number, use up every red canteen in the tribe, dust off The Dancing Girls. He'll never know what hit him. And when he wakes up, we'll be gone!"

"Rosie, . . . we're going to *leave* him?" Dad was shocked.

"It's him or us."

" . . . After forty years?"

"Exactly."

" . . . And when he wakes up in the morning . . . we'll be gone, . . . and . . . he'll be . . . all alone?"

"You got it." Mom folded her arms and planted her feet. "I'll make it easy on you men. I'm getting out tonight, and I'm going to take every woman and child in the tribe with me. You all can join us when you get tired hanging out."

Silence.

"I mean it," Mom said, "I'm through making circles in the sand."

Chapter Five

Mom started with the first tent she came to. She took the woman of the tent aside and whispered: "Sara and Joey are back. It's our P.L. all right, my brother Sid is there. And we're going down tonight—women and children first. Right after we all have a big party. Pass the word to the lady next door, and . . . and *don't tell Max*. We've got a surprise for him."

Mom was on her fifth tent when Norman and Benny caught up with her. They listened to her give the instructions; then Norman winked. "That's just fine, Rosie," he said, "thanks. We'll take over from here." The men weren't about to trade in Max as their leader for Rosie as their leader.

So the word was spread to the whole tribe. The next step was to con Max into a big party.

They worked the following trick: Norman and some other musicians started a loud argument in front of Max's tent. The scheduled evening entertainment was "New Song Night". Norman and the others pretended to fight over which one of them was going on that night.

They kept it up until Max came storming out of his tent. "Cut the fighting! You know I can't stand fighting! I run a smooth tribe."

"But, Max," someone said, "It's my turn tonight."

The others pitched in:

"No, my turn."

"No, *my* turn."

"But *I've* got a great new number."

"Hold it right there," Max said, "you've been around on that enough already. Now since you peons can't settle it—I'll settle it for you. You're *all* going on tonight! Every one of you!"

"But, Max," Norman whined, " . . . it'll take hours."

"Too bad, peons, you brought it on yourself. Go kill two sheep. You peons are going to dance tonight!"

And dance they did. And eat and drink and dance some more. The music never stopped—Max never stopped; and whenever he tried to slow down they spurred him on again, singing:

> "One more dance for Max everybody,
> Everyone up and circle around.
> Look at him go—a regular tiger,
> See his feet don't touch the ground!
>
> One more round for Max everybody,
> Clap your hands and keep that beat.
> Look at him go—a ninety-year wonder,
> See his flashy dancing feet!"

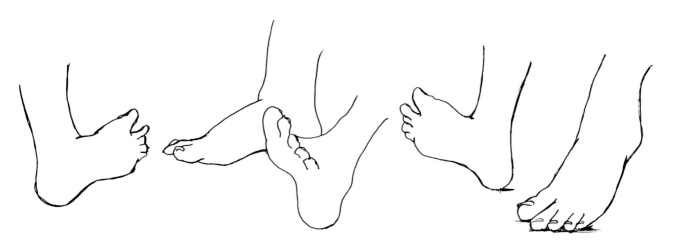

52

One More Dance

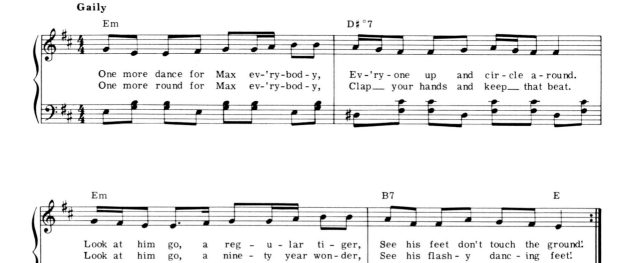

Gaily

One more dance for Max ev-'ry-bod-y, Ev-'ry-one up and cir-cle a-round.
One more round for Max ev-'ry-bod-y, Clap__ your hands and keep__ that beat.

Look at him go, a reg-u-lar ti-ger, See his feet don't touch the ground!
Look at him go, a nine-ty year won-der, See his flash-y danc-ing feet!

Then for good measure, they sent in The Dancing Girls, who danced old Max into his tent where they tickled and twirled him right out of his robe.

"YOU'VE HAD IT!" The Dancing Girls chorused.

"Oh, I have?" Max gasped. "Well, thanks, girls." And he curled up under the rug, and passed out.

53

Chapter Six

Quickly and quietly the tribe broke camp. At first, they decided to leave Max his camel and a tenth of everything else; but they raised his cut to a fifth because some people felt guilty about abandoning him.

When everyone and their donkeys and flocks were safely into the pass, they sealed up the entrance with boulders.

And Sara and Joey and Mom (on the camel) led the tribe toward The Promised Land.

The sun was high in the sky when Max stumbled out of his tent.

He stretched and scratched and yawned and rubbed his eyes.

He looked around.

He blinked.

He rubbed his eyes again, and looked around again.

And again!

He ran around the tent, looking in every direction.

Then he saw the pass was closed!

A slow smile broke across his ancient face.

His eyes twinkled.

He threw back his head and laughed.

Laughed!

Roared!

Raised his hands high to the heavens and howled!

Max brought out his favorite ram's horn. He blasted a few tunes off the cliff walls—so loud he could be heard far out in the wilderness.

Max had a leisurely breakfast. Then he took his flocks up on the plain to graze.

He saw a lone figure on a donkey a long way off to the east. Max played a few toots on the ram's horn, then sang out:

"Hey there! Hey there!

Are you going anywhere?

Hey there, my man,

Would you like a promised land?"

The man changed direction toward Max.

A couple appeared to the north. Max called to them:

"You two! You two!

How about a nice lamb stew?"

They headed Max's way.

It went like that all afternoon—Max singing his siren's song to the wandering strays and loners and little families. By dusk he had the beginnings of a tribe.

He led them all down to his camp, helped them with their tents, fixed them a fine feast. He made a great campfire. He told his best stories—stories about Spoof. Max was in rare form.

He sang them to sleep with his sweetest songs.

At first light, Max popped out of his tent:
>"Up now, my cousins,
>night is for sleep.
>Pack up your tents,
>round up your sheep."

He banged his frying pan.

>"I am your leader,
>That's how it has to be,
>Let's hit the trail now—
>Everybody follow me.
>>I'm only telling you,
>>what Spoof is telling me.
>>I'm only telling you
>>what He is telling me."

People straggled out of their tents.
They looked at Max like he was crazy.

>"He says to start looking
>for your promised land.
>I'll know what it looks like,
>—not too much sand.
>Some grass and some trees,
>and sometimes a breeze.

Max was getting to them.

"Your flocks will grow fat,
your numbers will soar,
your sons will grow tall
like I told you before.
I'm telling it clear,
I'm telling the truth—
Oh lucky the peons
been chosen by Spoof!"

People started running around, charged up. "That's good, that's right," Max said. "Pack up and we'll get going. Eat something first. Remember canteens."

Max walked through the camp checking out his new troops, trying to get the names straight. (He was having a little trouble with names these years).

Soon everyone was fed, packed, and assembled. Max got up on his camel. He looked to the sky and boomed, "OH SPOOF, OH SPOOF, . . . HERE THEY ARE." He closed his eyes. He seemed to listen. "Hmmm . . . hmm . . . ri-ight," he said.

Then Max looked back to the people: "Not too bad, not too bad, . . . *He's* not discouraged. He's seen worse. And anyhow, He's got nothing but time. Now let's move it! Let's hit the trail!"

Max pointed his camel east—east to the heart of the deep wilderness.

☆ ☆ ☆ ***THE END*** ☆ ☆ ☆